CLAY

CLAY

Poems by David Groff

*Winner of the 2012 Louise Bogan Award
for Artistic Merit and Excellence*

Groff, David
1st edition.

ISBN: 978-0-9855292-1-5
Library of Congress Control Number: 2012954359

Interior Layout by Lea C. Deschenes
Cover Design by Dorinda Wegener
Cover Art by Michael Brohman
Cover Photo by Clinton T. Sander
Editing by Terry Lucas and Dorinda Wegener

Printed in Tennessee, USA
Trio House Press, Inc.
Fernandina Beach, FL
Ponte Vedra Beach, FL

To contact the author, send an email to books@TrioHousePress.com

for Clay Williams

CLAY

THREE

ONE

CLAY'S FLIES

I pull Clay up behind a dune
and yank his bathing suit to his knees.
We are new together, at high tide.
But before I can sink to begin and Clay
could laugh and protest and rise,
the horseflies swarm,
the feast for them as good as a carcass.
They pepper his body like buckshot.
Clay yelps, thrashes me off him,
rushes to the ocean's fortress of breezes.

I watch him swell with *sixty-four* stings,
the beach of his body rising in red dunes
I cannot balm or even touch.
The flies divide us (what, you don't sting *me?*),
but the blisters betray his health:
his system rises with reprisals,
antivenin saturating the capillaries.

Time flies. Our lives fall into step together,
our sex indoors, the kisses typical.
Then the allergies abate: Clay hugs dogs,
roams dunes, breathes dust,
all mosquito bites a fading archipelago.
It isn't love that quells him,
it is HIV, its slowed but erosive work.
The bumps and sneezes that I feared
flicker out like fireflies in the fall.
Clay's skin shines as sharp as a whitecap,

deceptively dormant. I wish him welts.

This isn't 1984: the virus, we know, is manageable,
at least if you're the class of man who strolls
replenished beaches and has health insurance
and is lucky. Clay burned through all the drugs,
his veteran virus resistant to every trick but two,
an experimental pill he swallows without incident
and a powder he mixes in a vial with sterile water
and then aspirates and inserts in another vial and then
injects with exquisite slowness in a twist of skin.
He does this twice a day, goddamn it,
then rubs the bloat a quarter hour so it won't go hard
though as a rule it does— it sets into a smarting cyst,
a node, a pain in the ass, gut, arm, leg.

When his reachable sites go sore, I'm Clay's last resort:
I scrub, don latex gloves, and shoot him up
in some place his pinch-and-jab can't grab, forgetting,
in my rush to shrug away the nudge of death,
to grip his skin, or squeeze the needle one to twenty.
(How do the unmarried manage, doing this alone?
They use the clip for chip and pretzel bags.)
Then, as Clay has tutored me, I rub the sac, disseminating
the bite so that the blood subsumes it.
Strange to touch your man this way. A medicinal caress.

It works, for all its truculence. The t-cells we once
knew by name now rise to anonymity;
Clay sneezes like a demon all this spring.
I could lick his mucus like nectar.
As we make love like old explorers
nosing our sextants through the capes and beachheads,
my fingers linger on his every swelling,
the signal of another hour Clay will stay alive.
Later, lying leg to leg and chest to back,

I listen for the flies. Those jaded undertakers
twitch in the nearly hearable distance,
aching to make their mark amid the marks we make,
ready for my love's hot blood.

Clay's Face Is

a thinned blade
used hard,

scalpel and scalpel's
consequence,

boxers in the clinch,
squeezing out inessence

until blade or virus gasps,
respires.

His labial skin
swags him: the pills'

hateful miracle
strains fat.

He smiles:
the basset bounds.

He unsmiles: his face falls
but not in disappointment.

His head shows skull,
a study in bone,

honed to St. Jerome's
buzzkill pleasure.

He is wartime,
scorched earth,

his turf wasted
craters the generals' boys

die for. Its shrubs
inhale the smoke,

squirm for the sun,
root for fluid.

His eyes, the sentry's
lookout, look out:

he knows his face
is a trench afire.

He grins with all
his arrows of teeth,

he opens his mouth, he says
Stick out your tongue.

WHO IS HE

who steps out from the glare
in his slick white suit,
his tie and grin askew,
his shank of hair too?
In the slip of photo taupe
with time he is bare-
headed in the Upstate sun—
unlike the collared
and vested others,
severe and blinking—
his leg cocked, shoe or boot
divoting the hill,
eyes flashing wicked dark,
squinting. No, winking.

Make him the scamp son
of the chalky patriarch
knotted as a rope,
whom his hip infringes,
the bodiced lady his mother,
the turkey-necks his brothers—
a family stunned by sun
but solemn, and as wan
as if they guessed
their characters and names
are perditioned to the decades,
most text, all context
wizened into these shades
as browned as the hillside too
steep to pose on
long, its sky (gray here) the blue-
white of their dairy's cream—
on a Sunday after the sermon

he declined to listen to,
indulging the other
notions greasing
open the new century's hinges:
cereal, suffrage, sex.

He is all breath breathing
inside his louche suit,
his aroma the worm in
the tequila jar
he ate, New Orleans thieving,
Midland wildcat leasing,
Ruidoso land games,
the command hollered
down a canyon,
a new Olds car.
His stance strains the seam
of his ivory jacket.
He hates to have these clothes on
long, my raucous cousin;
he is charmed by sin.

I creep like a cricket
within
his linen.
I curl against his silk.
I rest
easy against his breast,
lick the Cuban cigar
in his scented pocket.
I forage into the thicket
of his wet chest,
I let
myself grip its thread,
the tonic of his sweat

sensational as milk.
I feel a risky chill.
I make my sighs guide him.
He pats me like a wallet,
steps away from the clan,
and spirits me inside him
down the dicey hill
past the homestead
into the white sun—
son, cousin, horizon—
our life begun.

HER GRAVE

Lancaster, PA 2003

No space here for Dave, just her and someday Dad
wedged in this double bed of grave,
waterproofed, judiciously unporous,
in their adjacent regulation crypts,
not exactly holding hands or sending cells
up to fertilize the apple tree that isn't here.
American ash stays ash and dust is dust.
But like the gilding of babyshoes
or the tussle for the bouquet,
this hygienic gesture soothes like chocolate,
the slightly startling resemblance to intimate bedtime,
still beneath closed lids. The occasional
visitors treading on her bedroom ceiling
in their New Balances, bearing mums and Evian,
stand solemn before her stone for entire moments,
until they die too, the marble sugars,
and the neglected granite groans with overexposure;
but even now all these *tabulae* are nearly *rasae*
of the crease and stink of human commerce:
love, alcohol, smarts with machines,
a taste for licorice or verbal abuse,
the curtained homosexuality or faith in God,
the tendency to give overlong directions
back to the main road out.
She lies in the *terra firma* of born and died,
sans crossword puzzles, disdain for Delaware,
an ear for the distinction between *who* and *whom*,
the five thousand school lunches made, altar linens ironed,

or whatever pain or surprise the wedding night compelled.
There are no apples. There is no tree.
As I say to Dad when he complains
that no one wants to listen to him grieve,
you can't go into a candy store and ask for meat,
you can't get blood from a stone.

My Father, a Priest, Pruning

East Orange, NJ

He painted the trunks with mud
to heal them, he said. They caked
as dark as the neighborhood's faces.
(I shame to compare them, but do.)

It worked; the wounds healed over,
the cherries scattered themselves
like spots of blood on the walks.
I tracked them to the church,

the bedroom floor, the bed
where I slept inhaling the taste
of fermenting cherry wine
he aged in the rectory basement

though I was not to tell
or say *He drinks* (it meant
He drinks too much
and he did not),

though I am telling now.
The sculpting of privets and trees,
the ivy regretfully ripped
from the church's porous bricks,

would open the property up,
keep muggers from lurking, he said,
allow the property light,
invite the people in!

It wouldn't work, I guessed:
the world and all its sins
would trespass onto our lot,
swipe my ball and bat,

because, I knew, we were white,
and they, like cherries, were black,
though often friendly and kind,
black sheep I saw as myself,

though others jumped me in school.
It didn't work, of course,
the whites all flew away,
the blacks prayed with themselves,

and my incredulous dad
kept clipping and pruning
God's little acre of turf
because aesthetics obtained

and hope persists like a stain.
The wine was spectacularly sour.
Gone now, trees and church,
the rectory, the mud,

supplanted by the hulk
of hospital next door.
My father, eighty-four,
refuses to admit

the church he labored for
exists just in his head
and I, at forty-six,
still fear the neighborhood.

I drink good wine for my heart.
Dad seldom drinks at all.
A single glass, and his face
goes red with the ruse of cheer.

CHANT

It reverbed beyond belief
to folk before the rood.
It colored the air like the glass.
The certifiers of God

pronounced it the sound of the soul
slipping the traces of plow,
promising great beyondness
beyond the sheep on the close.

The purified mouths of men,
the sound absent of organ,
the doubt of vibrato forgotten
like sketches of perspective,

exhort the stricken me
here in this beachside condo
that I was offered God
as naked before the window

I wrestle my angel of Clay,
their CD'd voices bleeding
their sated, unstained avowal,
to hell with my ocean howl.

Clay's Cough

The rasp of a tearing page
spasms from the living room.
As a mother knows her child's wail

instantly in a crowd,
I could sense through lead
his visceral breath—the cough

the boor who never leaves,
the spore we've had a threesome with
since September eleventh.

Today the hacking coincides
with a shift in wind excusing Staten Island
to insinuate the brimstone in our windows,

the incinerated Sheetrock, hard disc drives,
the powdered glass, bone, steel,
the hair and carpet fibers curling in the throat,

dusting our dinners with
a soupcon of electrical scorch, which
maybe is just a short on the Xmas tree.

It's like lilies rotting on the radiator,
the bums stale as towels, the falling clerks:
our senses blister. They flee town.

We swallow the cough. It's a jack-in-the-box.
It probably isn't September-infectious,
probably not the AIDS guerilla either.

Still, it shudders us both awake tonight—
tocsin, jester, cleaver of men.
Then we collapse suspicious into sleep.

To Men Dead in 1995

You recede into your dead millennium,
as remote as Reagan or Rommel.
Now that upscale men don't die en masse
& their disease has gone discreet,
your passion is antique, your shouts static.
You might as well have died in the towers,
another disaster students half-remember.

How embarrassing you embarrass me,
you with your absurd Doc Martens,
your shorts of hemmed denim,
the mimeoed leaflets blued to cloud,
your neckchains, your deadlines,
your youth with its squirmy whiff of Housman,
that brick of phone, the absence of tattoos,
your bad luck, your deconstruction,
the retro sideburns not yet retro now,
your young dumbness,
your skeleton of finger pointing,
your mouth sewn shut, your wirelessnessness.

HER CORPSE

Forget the devil in the details gotten wrong,
her sanguine fingernails and lips
seamed with God knows what adhesive,
the stink of carnations sprayed from a can
that you will never willingly inhale again,
her dearth of breath, brutal.
Allow her the praise the mourners offer:
So lifelike. So, lifelike. As if complimenting you.
As if she were a portrait you painted from life.
As if she only dozed in that sateen.

She lies there like Dorothy Gale asleep,
her suit her mother-of-the-groom original
in a dusty pink she didn't like in life,
favoring as she did theatrical shades,
her hands wax fruit facsimiles of hands,
their veins, you guess, plumped with a fluid,
her hair spun into auburn cotton candy,
her cheeks suspiciously firm,
though her forehead is nicely hard, secure
against your kiss, with its suggestion of skull.

If she rose up, as in the horror shows,
her necklace with its unclasped diamond cross
shivering toward her heart—you'd do what?
Resurrection is not on the marquee today.
But she's a cadaver you could carry around,
sling across your shoulder like a sack of fact,
steal past the minister's satchel of adages,
past Jack and Brenda Milton, David Earl,
past the Misses Shirley, Auntie Ruth,
the entire grieving, chatting crew,

and dance her delicious eggshell heft
into the Valentine's Day snows,
her pink wool flapping, her feet unslippered,
hair flecked with flakes and going straight,
a sleepyhead silent on your shoulder,
waltz her into the diner that she ate in last,
and sit her up smeared and warm,
all set to awaken from the storm
to tell you the most amazing bedside story.
But in whose balloon could you escape?

DREAD

Its chemistry husbands
each trifle into trauma:
the cane of the tear-shaped man,
the aspirin bottle skull,
a teen with scraped face.

Its merlins alchemize the cells
into a menu of lead
it serves as special of the day,
the diet of the psyche
deadlier than bread and water,

its concoction an occasion
to nourish an urge that rages
like soldiers stripping women
in the pillaged shopping mall,
dread the woman, dread the soldier.

JACKED

Farwell, TX toward Texico, NM

Driving late to the chain motel
past the empty lot of a town,
inhaling the feedlot reek,
plateaus of pulverized shit,
after seeing Clay's father
fresh from his lung scan
and his stepmother thinned
thanks to a third tumor,
we heard on the rental tires
an uproar of thud and crunch
akin to swallowing meat
as heard from within your head,
then something flicker or fly,
a sack or shooting star
that fled like a jackrabbit.
Jackrabbit, Clay remarked,
steering at ten and two,
steady on the gas.
My heart leaped into my head—
shouldn't we stop, should we
see what we hit?
I, a city boy,
always felt exempt
from corpses on the road
but Clay, of frontier stock,
let his father kill
his pet Raquel and her piglets
and ate pork within the year,
and saw his mother die
of one of the cancers the town

harvests like winter wheat.
The last of the gayboys
who slipped out and then returned—
the oldest to die of AIDS,
another to rev the car
to death in a closed garage—
he treats his blight of HIV
with ruthless pesticides.
Now he cruised into the night.
Jackrabbits die under tires.
The pioneer blood demands
and mile after mile requires
speed and brutal thrust.
At midnight in the high plains dark
as we plunged past the tracks
that separate the states
and mark a zone of time,
we gained an hour of life.

A BOY AND HIS GOD

1 What a Martyr

It is my mission only—
it is my only mission—
to rescue everyone ever
alive or dead.
Mom! I start with you. Ron!
Ms. Plath? Greg, are you down there?
Alfred the Great, collect yourself—
Paul, start your engines!

Empty the boardinghouses!
Evacuate the mausolea!

Mom! *Mom?*

Next? Pets.

2 *"Get Down off the Cross, We Need the Wood"*

Well, do you really? Unless you're resident of some truly
      treeless place, say outback, tundra, or the Upper East Side,
      don't you have other wood accessible, scrap or teak, even
      for free,
And while maintaining extra respect for old growth forests,
      92% of which in Minnesota have fallen for farmland, can
      I not justify 10 to 11 feet of 4x6's (okay, make it pine—it's
      the form that matters, not the content),
Even as I resent your tone of promiscuous cynicism, which
      has less to do with my sacrifice for, and redemption of,
      humankind than with your urge to remain an inert gas,
      accepting the low-expectation expectations of our post-
      holy age, while calamities, psychic adulteries, bad life-
      choices, and death ravish our privatized souls,
(Not to mention your louche use of a run-on sentence—
      replace the comma with a dash or semicolon after *cross* for
      God's sake),
So don't act so superior and blithe down there playing dice as
      my tendons splinter, drinking Cape Codders, sharpening
      your spear, and eyeing the sky for lightning—
Don't you ache not to die?

3 *Ex Post Facto*

You could always resort to the Mormons,
relying, after your last,
probably awful breath,
on the kindness of strangers,
i.e., some gung-ho descendent
in need of a belief system

in, say, 2091, who after
converting brings you along for the ride
and baptizes you into retroactive salvation,
grandfathering you in—
such a comfort for you dead who were content
to risk perdition ("a state of final spiritual ruin;
the future state of the wicked")—

and thus get your get out of jail free card,
comped into the planet's fastest growing faith
with admission to its 1964-World's-Fair-pavilion vision
of women with beautiful hairdos and puce robes
and their wet-combed husbands
greeting all you relieved arrivals
hefted into heaven on dry-ice clouds,
the afterlife an eternal choir recital
with the promise of fellowship hour beyond.
Here, have some bundt cake. Some punch.

This scenario assumes
(a) your grandkids are scared shitless and
(b) Joseph Smith was not a silly man.

4 *A Whole Day Not Thinking About God*

As if he decided to golf, the old man
in rayon shirt with his nipples showing through.
Or he doddered into the coffee shop,

sugar in his stubble,
too proud to ask directions,
a lame duck, still working the crowd.

Maybe his spittle, when he spoke, fell short
and so I didn't jerk around,
no stale-towel spray in my ear.

Or the dire ambulances
sirened over his summons,
and children shrieked.

At dusk I walk home like the rest of us,
divorcing, dithering over the body,
the stars' designs a set of disappointments,

when I miss the possibly homeless,
moldy magician with the holey cape
pull the dead rabbit out of his hat.

5 *Sexual Healing*

okay get ready this sex will be transcendent
a regular Shakespeare sonnet of deathless connection
my strokes and scansion such heav'nly eloquence
we'll be marqueed up into little stars
and we will make the face of heav'n so fine
we'll be like those lovers in that Japanese film
who kill themselves their love is so actualized
they will hear our joint Oh God
all the way to the cemetery *& back*
our universal love so individuated
the universe won't be decelerated
& kids stay kids oldsters creak not croak
lovers forever complain about their mates
okay this will be transcendent are you ready

TWO

Lost April

The pain of needing to pay so much damn attention
    devolves into deficit, distraction
with melting gutters revealed, the gossip of pigeons,
    and the rats lounging like bankers lunching
in the sun that shrugs into my squint as the planet tilts,
    my eyelids veined violet with it,
the mirrored sunglasses of stuff that keeps me from plunging
    my hand into the budded world's wound,
its flesh quick and provisional, its weeping redress
    a summons to roll away the stone and show a pulse
before everything appears: dead Mom's birthday, dead
    Ron's 45th, the early fruit, the litter spilling out.

We Boys Pull Down Our Pants

East Orange, NJ 1967

Chocolate, talcum, dirt, or unchewed bubble gum,
no matter our color we pulled them down,
extracted our rabbits out of hats
in the Marshalls' basement that reeked of greens.
Now we owned the toys our parents couldn't buy,
no batteries required: firemen's hoses,
puppets tumbling from their bunks as soldiers,
water pistols in dueling arcs of pee,
snails snaking into swords
we knew to bruise with
while upstairs, outside
the city darkened. Riots smoked the streets,
the Marshalls decided they were black,
the whites escaped like doves. Down below,
Jimmy Marshall's once-gray groin
went jet against my eggshell butt.
Warren looked and said it all was fucking queer.
Jimmy, Warren, David, Augustine, Lamont:
we saw we were a riot of colors,
boys inching into men,
becoming good at being hard.

Fancy Meeting You Here

You were supposed to be dead,
being missed for so long,
like the others another empty window
in a building blinking out. But there
you were in the Häagen-Dazs store,
seamed and thinned but
eating frozen yogurt, unlike a ghost.

Not that you and I had many minutes
remaining on our parking meter.
Your voice was still gut-deep
but full of nothing: lady gurus,
affirmations that kept you alive
(though they missed their shot
with the pessimistic dead...).

A dime of time and the red flag
flipped to the LED zeros
of your lovely eyes. You gave me
a dismissing kiss and ambled out
alive and now less precious
to the street of unmissing persons,
licking your globe of cone.

Fresh Pornography

I count his teeth, their niblets
of gold & black: I loll back
to conjure an episode with

him & a dentist, & assess
what he'd do for free.
A retainer revealed? I thrill to it.

I hit FF & he jackrabbits—
I let the coyote get him
squealing in silly terror:

I thresh his scene for a second
of spectacular rapture.
It never comes. He does.

He's no special guy.
A thousand men have
told me the same bedside story.

I rewind him to mystery & pants,
to freshen him like a drink:
some sloths yawn again.

But always he dies young.
In grief I run off with a grad
of the school of swollen tattoos.

I contemplate them like a god
too ADD to send only one son.
In the end I know them all

like I know the president.
Yet tin soldier after tin soldier,
they slay me over & over.

Their beards don't burn.
They do not scream in their sleep
& lack dangerous blood.

I pull up my socks.
I feel like a new man—
do you know any?

Rick O'Shea

Scanning my porn, with a view of the bay,
I hear a nasty thwack—
there on the designer deck
lies a catbird on his back
stunned or dead from the slab of glass

reflecting an IBM-blue sky
and trompe l'oeil pine,
limned as if in Chinese pen
or a Calvin model's scrim,
blind to the David and laptop within.

With his feet erect like a cartoon cat's
as if he toys at being dead,
I await his mean meow,
the clenching of his ruffled fist.
Nope. A fluid stains the slats.

I guess before my morning wank
I must spatula him up
and pitch him deep into the weeds
for dirt to undertake its work.
What tools do I have in the utility shack?

But first let me look at this electric pic
quivering on the screen,
with his nearly vinyl skin,
the bay his diode's diadem.
I wonder what is Rick O'Shea's real name.

Her Knee Surgery

There was I, deep in the hot tub convinced
I'd gotten God to rescue Mom
from the rogue clot. It was a persuasive
sensation, all the more winning because
I was naked, three hundred miles away
from her bedside, beside David Geffen's
night pines next door so etched & sexy
I knew I was alive, my groin boiling,
no limits on how long I could bubble.

She endured to circulate her legs
another eight years, but when she went
she died surprised, before I could
twist His arm, if He has an arm.
Dried, I survived & saw I was naked.
So much for the intercession of water
& pines sensate as saints. Geffen's house,
until a surgical strike or Operation Hurricane,
is owned now by lobbyists from Washington.

FIRE ISLAND SONG

It would be nice if you weren't dead,
you with your hair and skin flame-red
and your way of getting me in bed.
It would be nice if you weren't dead.

It's not time's fault or even fate's,
though this second claim demands debate:
Too many dead to live, you nearly said.
You savored dread.
You liked where it led.

You let death happen with your
drinks and drugs, your tour
of all the high points of despair.
You were a living cigarette.
You blistered and burned down. You let
me down. This grates.
This isn't fair,

I say, walking your beach beside myself,
your windy wispy ghost a stealth
seagull full of shit and caw.
You're also wind. You fuck me raw.

You like where I'm led.
You wanted me to die, you almost said.
The sunset is a scraped-skin red.
I would be nice if you weren't dead.

VODKA IN THE MORNING

is almost mistakable for mouthwash,
the stringent new day on your breath,

almost clean, like bleach or come,
almost bracing to kiss.

For me your shot nerves regroup,
shell-shocked soldiers rounded up,

your head armored against trembling.
You steady the chin I still see shiver.

I taste your dulled dread like a madeleine
almost sweet on the tongue:

when we were young and cool, highballing
like creatures out of Cheever,

when I found ice cubes spilled in your car
where you drank to steel yourself for me,

when if I only loved you enough you'd wake
and your breath would be grapes on the vine.

Paul Monette Has Left the Building

You ungowned yourself to show
the marvel of your swollen scrotum,
as if the jeweled egg you'd borne
from the Caucasus across the Elbe
smuggled cleverly in your pants
through Paris and past border guards
into the unsafe deposit of America
had suddenly blushed green
and grown more precious,
a scarab of remarkable powers
owned as it was by you.

Paul, you broadcast your death by inches
to governors and magazines,
performing your pinked rage,
dying no gentlemen's agreement,
no Episcopal fainting couch—
the courtier become the wizard
with his desiccant book of spells
the globe nodded slightly toward,
a ribbon wearing a hanging man,
vain, vain, and brave,
your flame so hot my face went red.

Yet when your final final assertion came,
your voice on the phone was a razor,
eerily virile—you'd forsworn all pills.
You'd write more soon, I promised—
that travel book we talked about—

No, you said, *I'm done*,
your matter all fact,
stripped for the sprint,
denying my denial,
your envoi sent.
I dropped the ball.

Edifice Complex

Maybe you died young because your dick was small.
You caressed it in the gym's shower stall, emerging
half-engorged & more like normal. Now I get why
you always tanned, incessant in your Speedo—so
your theater of perfect, alabaster ass would glow
as distracting as a followspot that you surmised
I kept churning like a moth to enter—no matter
the pills you tongued, the coke, the smoke, &
nerves & hot, brutal silence. Then your dark
came down like a velvet curtain that would
rise again for the concerto of frantic anger
you conducted, finally the maestro-artist
you ached to be. Your aspirations, they
rose as your true & fantastic erection,
designs of wild & rigid construction
I ventured into like a blasting zone.
& then your sad structure hushed.
Tears smeared your blueprint to
clouds; now I grieve our grief.
I didn't have the balls or dick
to rise to your high occasion,
& your cock shot far enough
to cleave my heart. Speared
by reckless panic & desire,
death-drugged, shadowed,
our last dance-last chance
let us eclipse ourselves.
Your light died in my
eyes. Going dark, a
spark flung out as
smoke, you felt
so small. Now
you are all.

LAST CALL

Frank, you deafen the dishes,
you sinuous drunk.
We can't hear ourselves plink.
You rout the garrulous host.
You outdrink us at this boite but
we slid in your scotch spit
on its picturesque steps.

Frankly you eat too much of our feta,
picking the best bits with pianist
nails you kiss with your pencily lips;
You smoke while you eat (ick),
your little penises of butts
an orgy of nerves these days
uncool as a dune buggy.

Time to go, great uncle, time
to throw down your liberty dimes
& sway back to your tenement
so we can clear the air,
& eat your share.
Oh Frank we love you get out.
Don't fret, we'll call in the AM.

MILTON

Not the poet—though yes,
a poet, aspiring. Old.
At Big Cup he regards us
slickened with testosterone,
his eyes entertained.
Though his full hair helps him
seem a youth in drag
save for the swags of his neck,
he can't but help present
himself as age itself,
a brand of birthmark
we think we won't accrue,
unnerving as June rime
limning a suburban lawn.
His melting candle of body,
cupped, burns. He grins.

Compare him to the man-crone
trolling Our Place
in Des Moines with Frank
Fortuna and Dan Grace
two decades ago:
Brutally cruising, drunken,
his halo of hair aflame,
he swaggered to budding men
declaring *You'll be me!*,
his annunciation denunciation,
then stalked off, sated.
The boys, abashed and angry,
decided time was a virus
you just had to swallow.
The faggot angel of death,

Frank baptized him.
Now Frank is fifty-one,
commences drinking at noon.

Maybe knowing Frank,
or himself an initiate of crones,
and warhorse of Village cafes
whose soldiers now are wraiths,
(who here knows
what old men know?),
Milton acts like he belongs.
He steps among tattoos,
buzzed hair, and bashful mouths,
inhales the caffeine and finds
himself an appropriate chair,
surveying the sipping guys,
while taking care to seem
a clean old man.
He winks, to summon us
to the fallen fruit of himself
that if we've got gut enough
we will pick up and eat.

Dead AIDS Poet Archive

Their Corrasable datedness glares:
the Berlin Wall. Cassettes.
Vice President Bush. KS.

Fusty in their acidic folders
they are too gay and grim to
snare you like Berryman or Clare.

Instead they just lie there,
knights embedded in sarcophagi,
members of inscrutable orders.

Even their Xeroxed pics—
Tracy's voluptuous mullet,
David's mouth of mustache,

the roses of Glen's shirt,
Jim's throat's scaly matte—
padlock their cabinets.

Still. Those smudged serifs,
the grain of their onionskin,
the square Courier of their

type faces beckon
you to lie down with them.
They say *Read us in bed.*

HER FINGERPRINTS ARE

everywhere invisible
but if you cast the right dust
they will ghost
on that sherry glass,
the cat's vaccination medal,
the vial of Ambien.

Look for her thumb
in her own mother's thimble,
the moist arc on
my father's teacup
and six Kisses' wrappers,

a scrap of a whorl
at the bevel of her pencil
and her mark oiling my
last boy-picture.

They rise to light
like a body breaking
the veil of river.

Unlid the cold cream:
her last night's last swipe.

—Don't touch it, don't
probe. No, wait,
Let me go first.

SCAVENGER

Yes, like this gull
buzzing the fishing boat,
teased out to sea
too far to fly
if he could not light
on the scaly deck,
lured by guts
the world splits open,
improbably white,
taking to heart
the free debris
and worthless fish,
the castaway who
refuses no refuse,

or this vulture
eying the dying,
patroller of roads,
a hungry undertaker,
savoring stink
the others shirk,
beyond disdain,
doing a favor,
the desert shadow
unflappably there,
no predator but
the death of the party,
his claw an embrace,
his eye on the sparrow.

THREE

CLAY

Sedona, AZ, December 24

Too late in the day, we climb the cliff,
the snow rusty with mud, the rocks' tread slick,
up Sugarloaf Trail, up Teacup's switchbacks,
up Summit Trail, a sliding board,
scooping in breath after breath—
Clay deft as a coyote, outstripping
me in my black Prada sneakers,
suspicious of the sun, summoning
the specter of Robin Hardy 200 miles south
who in the desert dusk took a shortcut
that skittered him into a bowl of death.
With antivirals, he'd persist today, like Clay.
I prod the five-alarm fuss of my heart.

Clay sways at the crest, surveys the sheer drop.
Below him, Sedona purples.
I hang back, breath staticky, my Prada terra cotta.
I peer at the cheeseboard of Sedona,
its dressed-for-Xmas adobe abodes erected
out of plywood in the Reagan reign,
its pools a banquet of robin's eggs.
Some upstanding hippie citizens believe
these rocks garage a UFO, a cosmic cavalry
come to save us from ourselves—
let the horsemen spirit in a crystal pill
or spin time's desert back, to give me
Robin unfallen and Clay a safer 20.

"Amazing what the oceans do," Clay breathes.
The cliffs, football-orange, seamed with snow,

convoke before us like faces of O'Keeffe.
Sea-scraped, scratched into scales,
wind-ripped, seared, their vertebrae exposed,
they rose as maidens, all curves and seaweed,
to become this witchery of ridges
concocting meaning like a Christmas brew.
Robin knew. On that cold feverish night,
broken on the steep of desert, before Ted
crept away at dawn and found a phone,
he went on about the Wendigos,
the Bigfoots and Abominables,
and the errant Hero Twin the Monster Slayer,
skulking in whatever your native wilderness,
who makes all scary creatures turn to dust.
Robin slid and died before Ted made it back.

The valley's reddened eyes go glassy.
I squint at the grimacing crones
so beautifully immune to imploration,
nothing in their ores but more geology.
Rocks are rocks. The rust is iron oxide.
I think I hear the Sedona TV Network
broadcast extensive holiday blessings
as TV has-been Glenn Scarpelli banshees
O Holy Night into an evening wholly empty

yet Clay hears nothing but sunset.
His eyes, more sharp than mine,
fall onto a far-off face:
the Lone Ranger and his crusty friend
mountain-goat it up the cliff,
scouts sent to soothe the ladies' sunburn,
calming them enough to let
the jumpy natives sleep all Christmas Eve.
It's actually two raptors.
They unfurl their flags and rise

to sketch the message of themselves.
My feet are so cold. I step ahead a bit.
Clay's scarp of face is raw as clay.
My cellphone bleats.
The earth arcs left,
at our soles the vacant
air of precipice:
we edge close.

LOVE POEM

Ben and Fella stand head to butt
to use their tails to brush the flies
from each other's snout and eyes.

It almost works, their deal, but
still it happens that the flies
suck the nectar from their eyes.

SAME OLD SAME OLD

How to exonerate the second fart in bed,
the bed reciting the same damn yarns,
the boring penis boring the cored, chapped ore,
the hairs curled, fetal, beside a shot glass,
the tits once pert as toddlers drooped like dough,
the spectacles oral sex demands, the face age clawed,
the shared first pets as dead as parents,
the embers gray enough to grasp?
—The bed's a leaky raft. Swallow the fart,
clutch the cock at its base like a fading pen,
espouse the other, later body like a dated cut of coat,
holes rent in every solitary pocket,
its cool coals dropped like change on the street
for bums and kids to find and spend.

The Tomb of Lysias

after Cavafy

I have passed my twenty-third summer
in the Beirut library, roofless now,
after the troubles with the Christians.
The last librarian, I can't recall his name,
the one who smokes those little gray cigarettes,
is gone and they've got a new one, a woman.
Few books have been destroyed so far
in the shelling, so my reading is unhindered—
except for that beautiful gentleman, Rami,
who works near my desk and seems himself
a source of sunlight. Before the worst of the heat
sometimes, we slip out to the old wrecked lobby
and, seated on a slab with its letters rubbed clean,
crack open pecans on the stone, and talk,
until mortars and our own shyness
pull us back to the splintered corridors.

MUSCALURE

Fat fly, ripe as a grape,
your eyes a thousand spies,
you cruise me, you grope,

you hone your fecal nails,
you rub your palms—sleek
villain, me roped to your rails—

too sly to be a bullseye as I
slap myself silly to still you, you
with your eye for the faux-blasé

clandestine caress, your
bait & twitch of insinuation,
the spark of my shivering, your

kiss like a silk of his hair
that stealths the pillow to my throat,
the eyelash triggered on my ear,

his breath a stiletto in my eye.

BING

Oh that was delicious
I say, biting
into the blued ruby,
a gunshot of flavor
at its bloodiest climax—

and realize I am still
eating it, the past
tense a reflex
of scarcity, of
overfed grief even

in the savoring, nothing
but indulgence.
                    Past
the glass the day
glares, greens,
mostly pistils & shoots.

POWER FAILURE

Dusk inches in,
like it or not.
Lost to current,
you make do how
birds do—make
final calls & subside.
The sun's bugs sleep.
Fireflies are no help.
Fickle, they flicker,
elude your dark jar.
The cows, all stomachs
full enough, kneel
& lie in somnolence,
their hides resistant
to mosquitoes, unlike
yours. Moths lack
your bright bulb
to die against. You
too spin free of
such obsessional
inventions. Intentions
lose their spark.
Your charge gives in
to the turning world
that gutters out to
sleep like a baby.
Sleep, baby,
your light is night.

PLASTIC FLOWERS

True to their artifice,
they weather weather.
They resist the rain,
they suffer sun;
wind-careen down the curve
does not denude them.
Bees don't drain them.
Their petals petroleum
like the road's macadam,
they are akin to the engines
and cries of tires
that called them here
to their *descansos*.

They offer the road a cross,
its edges bloody with clay,
and stakes of bouquets
as if planted in the gravel,
ribboned with loss:
Beloved Jennifer, Estimados Jose y Jocelyn,
Kevin Alive in Our Hearts,
Pedro no esta perdido, Cayden Never Forgotten,
like wreathes for racehorses.

The sun leisurely bleaches them:
the blues grow bruised,
the reds rose.
The roses relax into carnations
pink as clay. The carnations
unclench and go gray.

Their banners fray.
Words whiten.
Frost. Whips of wind.
They degrade with the road
and the shoulder, and sooner;
they suffer the scythe
of the semis' shed treads,
a drunken pickup,
and everyday cars
that fail to slow to see
the sprays, as commonplace
as mileposts, coyote carcass,
the strayed, swaying skidmarks.

Petals trembling on their stems,
they quiver like flowers
paled to flesh,
facsimiles of clay,
the thumbs of children
hoping to hitch a ride.

Her Dream Weekend

I bring her to the beach she never saw alive.
She is holding my hand with her wedding ring hand
so hard she crushes my carbon to diamond.
As long as the sun plunges
we lie here chaise by chaise
eating the crudités I made,
sipping the sweet white wine she craves,

rendered as new as the weird old couple
retrieving beach debris.
The saline wind with its whips
and the waves with their edgy goodbyes
say our skin is surging with life.
They dry our eyes.

We make the best of it
as anti-day discovers us
and turns us into pillars of salt
because I turned around to get her—
I couldn't take no for an answer.

Keep Dreaming

I tackle him demanding he stop being dead—
C.S. Lewis dirging Joy, Paul keening Rog,
the Sati bride astride the husband's fiery pyre—

& Clay sits up to give a jack-o'-lantern grin:
"Can't I just not go today?" What a drag.

Flashbulb pop: my eyes crust open, I see ceiling,
then his gray used head & body asprawl beside me,
feet snared in the sheets, his length a felled birch blooming.

So strikingly not dead or even appearing ready to go,
meds still simmering, pulse ticking, breath occurring.

Essay, for Clay

Eat me not like a coyote
shaking the dog's dead neck,
then shot by the hunter,
coyote as compost;

snap me like a sunflower,
enough for a hundred blackbirds
and the scythe of wind
to seed the landfill,

crack me open
in your incisors,
let my oils
assume your saliva,

shake my stalk,
plant your mouth
against my dinner plate:
I erupt multitudes

for you, I am Abraham's stars.

YOUR GUST

This dead summer
afternoon summons you—
you would hate today
if you were alive,

your July laden, fetid,
vacation an exile
from flowered china, linen,
air conditioners, an easy bath.
You crossed off days
until you returned to life.

—At the campsite rife
with your husband's eden,
you pick your way among
the tent stakes straining,
the flypaper snared on a pole,
and the cats' leashes,
to stab the ice chest's
slick, impossible block
into daggers for a drink,
the creases in your arms
adhesive in the heat,
your snood of hair pulled up
into a hateful kerchief
to lift it half off your neck,
the spine of your Graham Greene
split on the oilcloth.
Sweat beads your powder.
You straighten up,
and at that second

as just now

it pierces the pines—
the grace of gust.
A surveyor sighing,
a spy for fall,
the whisper of a New Year's gown.
You tilt your chin like a cat,
raise your mane from your neck,

and in the present past of July
you exhale
a breath of air.

What's the Matter

As I lie dead on the hillock,
    an open invitation,
        my carcass garbage,

the vultures unashamed
    dive into their meal,
        a method to their madness.

They open their teeth of beaks.
    I feel them catch in my throat
        & share my callus of liver.

They score beneath my ribs
    to get to the heart of the matter.
        They must work to pick my brain.

My penis for them isn't hard.
    They mean to be only vultures—
        I am a beggar's banquet.

Finished, I stick in their craws
    as we take to the bed of the sky.
        We rise and shine.

EPITHALAMION

to Clay

After the mutual cruise in the surf,
after I ignored the fact your towel was pink,
after the hellos, the wind tousle, the shifting
to face each other now sitting on the pink towel,
after I swallowed that you attended seminary—
damn, you're my goddamn father, damn—
after I decided that was interesting,
after I said, testing but not expecting,
(you were younger, you were Texan,
exiled from the early scourge of HIV),
AIDS was such a bummer &
you looked at me deadeyed & said you had it,
after my heart sank & bobbed up again
because your face grew richer in the evening beachlight,
& because you were not the first of my men to be mortal
(thank you Craig, Jay, Ron, Len, Paul,
all of you dead by then, my bruised test cases),
because you laughed like a little boy
at the cartoon plovers skittering the sand,

after we went back to your room & did everything but it,
after the two weeks of phone calls before you returned to my island,
after the sighting of you at the ferry dock & my shock
at the face I'd half-forgotten, its pockmarks & wine-dark eyes,
after the heat lightning on the beach that flashed at us like
    God's metaphor,
after the urgent clumsy love,
after we were careful for the first of a thousand times
& we opened the doors to ourselves & the same wind blew through,

on the day we went to Washington for the Quilt
& I saw you as part of that carpet,
at the healing service where the bishop anointed you with oil
& I was blasted open with tears
& you were blasted open with tears,

I could do nothing but marry my life with death,
to the coded body of life in death
& the moment the wind will blow us apart,

the embodied air of you, the promise of absence,
the robust receding wave
the moon takes back, to leave behind an ocean.

Notes

1. Page 34, title: "Get Down off the Cross, We Need the Wood" is from the 1996 debut album from the band Firewater, entitled *Get off the Cross, We Need the Wood for the Fire*.

2. Page 35, lines 12-13: "a state of final spiritual ruin;/the future state of the wicked" is the definition of "perdition," word for word from Dictionary.com.

3. Page 36, title: "Sexual Healing" is the title of the 1982 song recorded by Marvin Gaye.

ACKNOWLEDGMENTS

Some of these poems have previously appeared in these
periodicals:

The American Poetry Review: "The Tomb of Lysias"
The Awl: "Fire Island Song"
Barrow Street: "Chant," "Lost April"
Bloom: "Milton"
Court Green: "Her Knee Surgery," "Last Call"
Great River Review: "Who Is He" and "Your Gust" as ("My
    Mother's Gust")
Inkwell: "We Boys Pull Down Our Pants"
The Iowa Review: "My Father, a Priest, Pruning"
Mead: "Vodka in the Morning"
Meridian: "Her Grave"
Phati'tude: "Same Old Same Old"
The Promethean: "Muscalure"
Seven Carmine: "Clay's Cough," "Rick O'Shea"

"Her Grave" received the 2005 Editor's Award from *Meridian*
magazine.

My thanks to the Anderson Center for Interdisciplinary
Studies, Hall Farm, Hidden River Arts, the Kimmel Harding
Nelson Center for the Arts, the Ragdale Foundation, the
Saltonstall Foundation, the Santa Fe Art Institute, the Virginia
Center for the Creative Arts, and Wilderness Retreat for the
time and space to work on these poems.

My thanks to all to helped bring the poems in this book to
light, especially Linsey Abrams, Jan Beatty, Michael Brohman,
Jan Crawford, Jim Elledge, Alan Felsenthal, Charles Flowers,
Jameson Fitzpatrick, the Reverend Addison Keiper Groff, Irene
Bornemann Groff, Jonathan Groff, Christian Gullette, Robert
Hedin, Walter Holland, Timothy Liu, Marie Ponsot, Kelly

Rowe, Elaine Sexton, Aaron Smith, Rob Weisbach, and my poet colleagues at theurbanrange.com.

My thanks to Michael Waters and my editors at Trio House Press.

All love and gratitude to Clay Williams.

About the Author

David Groff lives in New York City. His book *Theory of Devolution* was selected by Mark Doty for the National Poetry Series. With Philip Clark, he edited the anthology *Persistent Voices: Poetry by Writers Lost to AIDS*. With Jim Elledge, he edited *Who's Yer Daddy?: Gay Writers Celebrate Their Mentors and Forerunners*. He completed the book *The Crisis of Desire: AIDS and the Fate of Gay Brotherhood* for its author, the late Robin Hardy. An independent book editor, he teaches in the M.F.A. in Creative Writing Program at The City College of New York.

About the Artist

Michael Brohman is an artist and educator based in Denver, CO. He holds a Masters of Architecture degree from the University of Colorado Denver and an undergraduate degree in Design and Ceramics from Colorado State University. He is on the faculty at the University of Colorado Denver as a Senior Instructor of Sculpture. He has also taught sculpture in Scotland, Ireland, and China.

Michael has had numerous solo exhibitions and his work has been recognized with an Artist Fellowship from the Colorado Council on the Arts. Michael has participated in artist residency programs at the Jentel Foundation and the Santa Fe Art Institute.

About the Book

Clay was designed at Trio House Press through the collaboration of:

Terry Lucas, Lead Editor
Clinton T. Sander, Cover Photo
Michael Brohman, Cover Sculpture: *Baptism*
Dorinda Wegener, Cover Design
Lea Deschenes, Interior Design

The text is set in Adobe Caslon Pro.

The publication of this book is made possible, whole or in part,
by the generous support of the following individuals and/or agencies:

Anonymous

About the Press

Trio House Press is a collective press. Individuals within our organization come together and are motivated by the primary shared goal of publishing distinct American voices in poetry. All THP published poets must agree to serve as Collective Members of the Trio House Press for twenty-four months after publication in order to assist with the press and bringing more Trio books into print. Award winners and published poets must serve on one of four committees: Production and Design, Distribution and Sales, Educational Development, or Fundraising and Marketing. Our Collective Members reside in cities from New York to San Francisco.

Trio House Press adheres to and supports all ethical standards and guidelines outlined by the CLMP.

The Board of Directors of Trio House Press would like to thank Lindsay Small-Butera.

The Editors of Trio House Press would like to thank Michael Waters.

CPSIA information can be obtained at www.ICGtesting.com
Printed in the USA
BVOW030404200213

313706BV00002B/21/P